Comprehension Mini-Lessons

Inference & Cause and Effect

**by LeAnn Nickelsen
with Sarah Glasscock**

NEW YORK • TORONTO • LONDON • AUCKLAND • SYDNEY
MEXICO CITY • NEW DELHI • HONG KONG • BUENOS AIRES

SCHOLASTIC
Teaching
Resources

I would like to thank the following people for this book:

my husband, Joel, and my twin children, Keaton and Aubrey, for encouraging and supporting me with the goal of writing this book.

my parents, Jim and Dolores Heim, for helping me with ideas and for all their support. Thanks Mom and Dad for creating the "Who Am I?" activity.

Virginia Dooley, my senior editor, for helping me become a more concise writer and for all of the writing opportunities she has given me.

Sarah Glasscock, my cowriter, and Sarah Longhi, my editor, who spent numerous hours checking over this book to make sure it was perfect.

my sister, Sherry DeVilbiss, for being a great, supportive friend. I know you really wanted your name to be in a book, so here it is (hahaha).

my education friends who have taught with me through the years. You know so much and have contributed so much time and effort. You know who you are!

Grapevine-Colleyville ISD in Texas for supplying me with resources and advice. Anne Simpson, your knowledge is valued by many. Thanks for the help with summarization and main idea.

—LeAnn Nickelsen

Cover design by Norma Ortiz

Cover art by Shari Warren

Interior design by Sydney Wright

Interior illustrations by Teresa Southwell

Contents

Introduction

The *Comprehension Mini-Lessons* Series

National and state standards, and schools across the country require all students to master a set of reading objectives, with an emphasis on these key comprehension areas: main idea, summarizing, inference, cause and effect, point of view, fact and opinion, sequencing, and context clues. For me and the teachers I work with, teaching students to deepen their comprehension has always required several creative lessons for each reading objective to ensure that everyone achieves success. Customizing each lesson plan is a lot of work, and that's where this series of high-interest mini-lessons—designed from years of classroom lesson successes—comes to the rescue.

Each book in this series provides you with several different mini-lessons for each objective, which appeal to different learning styles and help you reach each and every learner. The mini-lessons include activities and real-world examples so that students have fun learning the reading objective and find the skills they learn useful in their everyday reading and pertinent to their lives.

About This Book

This book presents lessons that teach students skills and strategies for understanding inference and cause and effect.

Inference

Inferring is the act of reading between the lines—predicting or guessing what is going on when it is not actually explained in the writing. If authors explained everything that happened and didn't allow us to make inferences, we wouldn't have much to think about and books would be ten times longer than they really need to be. Readers make meaning by evaluating the author's words to draw conclusions about the story or subject and create logical predictions about what might happen. Readers who build skills in sequencing can visualize events, make sense of a story line, predict what may happen based on the time and order of events in a story, and better understand the causes and effects of events.

Cause and Effect

Understanding how causes bring about effects is crucial to making good decisions in life. If we do *this*, then *that* could happen. Acting on our understanding of consequences—how our actions create helpful or unhelpful situations—is part of surviving and getting along in a community. When we realize that there are consequences that are related to our actions, we become more cognizant of and responsible for our behavior. Readers who recognize

cause-and-effect relationships in stories or nonfiction texts can make predictions and learn from characters' choices.

How to Use This Book

You'll find five mini-lessons on inference and six mini-lessons on cause and effect with activities that stimulate different learning styles (visual, auditory, and kinesthetic). I recommend teaching all of the lessons sequentially. The first lesson introduces the objective in simple terms. The next few lessons elaborate on the objective and offer students different skills to better understand it. The last lesson features the objective in a standardized-test format, which helps familiarize students with the test language and structure. A final project pulls the whole concept together and offers students an opportunity to demonstrate creatively what they learned in the mini-lessons. Students also get to share their learning with other classmates when they complete a project. Whenever students teach other students what they have learned, the learning becomes more cemented in their brains.

Notice that each lesson contains anticipatory sets, which enable you to grab students' attention when you open the lesson, and special closures to end the lesson so that students' brains can have another opportunity to absorb the learning. Also included are activities that you can send home to extend the learning in another real-world setting.

—LeAnn Nickelsen

Young Adult Fiction Resources

In addition to the excerpts from literature that you'll find in the lessons, here are some additional suggestions for young adult literature that supports the objectives in this book:

Books that support making inferences

Adler, David. *Cam Jansen Adventures*. New York: Viking, 1980.

Dalgliesh, Alice. *The Courage of Sarah Noble*. New York: Simon & Schuster Children's Books, 1986.

DeClements, Barthe. *Nothing's Fair in Fifth Grade*. New York: Puffin Books, 1990.

Gilson, Jamie. *Itchy Richard*. New York: Clarion Books, 1991.

Books that feature cause-and-effect relationships

Hader, Berta & Elmer. *The Big Snow*. New York: Macmillan, 1948.

Howe, James. *Bunnicula*. New York: Windrush, 1989.

Moore, Lilian. *Don't Be Afraid, Amanda*. New York: Macmillan, 1992.

Myers, Walter Dean. *Fallen Angels*. New York: Scholastic, 1988.

Inference

Inference Charades

Opening the Lesson

✤ To begin this lesson, I pretend to be exhausted. Without speaking, I perform the following actions: walking sluggishly to my desk, rubbing my eyes, stretching my arms overhead, yawning several times, and slumping into my chair.

✤ Usually my students stare at me (and sometimes each other) and wonder what's going on.

✤ Then I spring up energetically and ask them what kind of mood I just displayed, and how they could tell. My students respond that I seemed tired or sleepy and that they could tell by my body language. Then I say, *"Oh, so you* inferred *that I was tired by the physical clues I gave you."*

✤ Write the following definitions of *inferring* on the chalkboard:

- making an assumption based on subtle verbal and nonverbal clues
- judging or concluding that something is true
- analyzing facts and coming to a logical outcome based on the evidence
- drawing conclusions (reading between the lines)
- realizing "Oh, now I get it!"

Also point out that inferences may be used to predict what might logically happen next. Discuss which elements of the definition your students used to determine that you were tired.

Teaching the Lesson

1. To prepare, cut out the words on the Charade Strips reproducible, fold the strips in half, and place them in a bowl or paper bag.

2. Group students in pairs. Tell them that they'll be playing a game of charades to strengthen their inference skills. Explain the rules of the game:

- Without peeking, one partner draws a charade strip. Both partners read the action and discuss quietly how to act it out. (If they're not sure what the word means, they can look it up in the dictionary.)

Objective

Students define inference and give examples. They infer actions or feelings by playing charades.

Materials

scissors, bowl or paper bag, dictionary

Reproducibles

Charade Strips, page 9 (Make 1 copy.)

Inferential Reflection Sheet, page 10 (Make 1 copy per student.)

- Each partner takes a turn performing the action for the rest of the class for about one minute. Then students in the audience raise their hands to guess the action. Partners call on students until someone guesses correctly. If a synonym is given instead of the exact word on the charade strip, partners signify this by drawing an *S* in the air. The audience must brainstorm other synonyms until they say the exact word.

3. When the game is over, discuss how playing it reflects the definition of *inferring* that you wrote on the board.

4. Of course, making inferences can be trickier than playing a game of charades. I broach this by saying, *"Why do we need to spend time learning how to infer? I know it seemed easy when we played charades, but in real life it's not always that easy."* Read aloud the examples below to show your students how easy it can be to make incorrect inferences.

    a. At the beach, Taylor saw a sign that read

      SHARKS

      NO SWIMMING.

    Taylor inferred that sharks were not allowed to swim in this area. What did the sign really mean?

    b. Antonio came home from school and didn't say a word to anyone. Antonio's mom saw him run into his room and heard the door slam behind him. She got angry because she inferred that Antonio was being disrespectful to her by slamming his door. She raced into Antonio's room and was about to ground him when she realized his window was open and a strong breeze was blowing. What could Antonio's action have meant?

Closing the Lesson

Use one or more of these activities to wrap up the mini-lesson.

✿ **Assessment:** Have students complete the Inferential Reflection Sheet reproducible. Guide students who are having trouble by prompting them with questions. (NOTE: They will use these completed sheets in Mini-lesson 2.)

✿ **Students Working Together:** Have students pair up to create their own examples of incorrect inferences. Set aside class time for your students to present their examples.

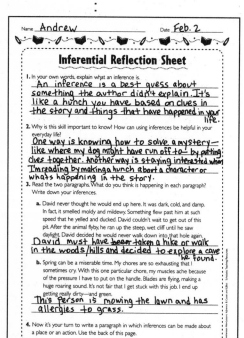

Name Andrew   Date Feb. 2

Inferential Reflection Sheet

1. In your own words, explain what an inference is.
An inference is a best guess about something the author didn't explain. It's like a hunch you have based on clues in the story and things that have happened in your life.

2. Why is this skill important to know? How can using inferences be helpful in your everyday life?
One way is knowing how to solve a mystery— like where my dog might have run off to— by putting clues together. Another way is staying interested when I'm reading by making a hunch about a character or what's happening in the story.

3. Read the two paragraphs. What do you think is happening in each paragraph? Write down your inferences.

  a. David never thought he would end up here. It was dark, cold, and damp. In fact, it smelled moldy and mildewy. Something flew past him at such speed that he yelled and ducked. David couldn't wait to get out of this pit. After the animal flyby, he ran up the steep, wet cliff until he saw daylight. David decided he would never walk down into that hole again.
David must have ~~been~~ taken a hike or walk in the woods/hills and decided to explore a cave he found.

  b. Spring can be a miserable time. My chores are so exhausting that I sometimes cry. With this one particular chore, my muscles ache because of the pressure I have to put on the handle. Blades are flying, making a huge roaring sound. It's not fair that I get stuck with this job. I end up getting really dirty—and green.
This person is mowing the lawn and has allergies to grass.

4. Now it's your turn to write a paragraph in which inferences can be made about a place or an action. Use the back of this page.

10

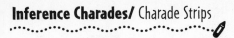
To the teacher: Cut the strips along the dotted lines. Fold the strips in half, and place in a bowl or a paper bag. You can add more words on the blank strips.

embarrassed	exhausted
frightened	bored
disappointed	thrilled
worried	desperate
uninterested	frustrated
puzzled	shy
surprised	lonely
overwhelmed	relaxed
clueless	joyful
lucky	loved
diligent	stressed out
pondering	optimistic

Inferential Reflection Sheet

1. In your own words, explain what an inference is.

_____

_____

_____

_____

2. Why is this skill important to know? How can using inferences be helpful in your everyday life?

_____

_____

_____

_____

3. Read the two paragraphs. What do you think is happening in each paragraph? Write down your inferences.

   a. David never thought he would end up here. It was dark, cold, and damp. In fact, it smelled moldy and mildewy. Something flew past him at such speed that he yelled and ducked. David couldn't wait to get out of this pit. After the animal flyby, he ran up the steep, wet cliff until he saw daylight. David decided he would never walk down into that hole again.

_____

_____

   b. Spring can be a miserable time. My chores are so exhausting that I sometimes cry. With this one particular chore, my muscles ache because of the pressure I have to put on the handle. Blades are flying, making a huge roaring sound. It's not fair that I get stuck with this job. I end up getting really dirty—and green.

_____

_____

4. Now it's your turn to write a paragraph in which inferences can be made about a place or an action. Use the back of this page.

Comprehension Mini-Lessons: Inference & Cause and Effect   Scholastic Teaching Resources

The KIS Strategy

Opening the Lesson

❦ To begin this lesson, I read aloud Shel Silverstein's book *The Giving Tree* to my students and then ask them the following questions about the book:

How do you feel about the tree?

How do you feel about the boy?

Why do you think the tree kept giving to the boy?

Did the boy give back to the tree?

What can we learn from this book?

What inference can you make about this book that will help you live a better life?

❦ It's important to point out that not everyone will conclude the same thing about the book. This will allow you to introduce the concept of the KIS strategy to your students. Here is what I usually say to my class:

We come from various backgrounds and have a wide range of experiences that cause us to make inferences in different ways. But, even though we may draw different inferences, we're all using the same strategy! This strategy has three parts: one—remembering the key words or facts from the text; two—making inferences by using the key words or facts to fill in missing information; and three—being able to support those inferences with facts and our personal experiences. This strategy is called the KIS strategy.

> **Tip**
>
> I make a poster of the KIS strategy steps on page 14 to display in the classroom.

Teaching the Lesson

1. Hand out copies of the KIS Strategy reproducible to your students. Go over the three steps of the strategy:

Objective

Students use a mnemonic strategy to make and support inferences about short passages.

Materials

The Giving Tree by Shel Silverstein (HarperCollins, 1964) or a similar book, completed Inferential Reflection Sheets from Mini-Lesson 1, poster-board, markers

Reproducibles

KIS Strategy, page 14 (Make 1 copy for each student or 1 poster or transparency.)

KIS Strategy Examples, page 15 (Make 1 transparency.)

Practicing the KIS Strategy, page 16 (Make 1 copy for each student.)

K – Key words (Underline key words or facts that will help you make an inference.)

I – Infer (Use the key words to guess what information is missing from the text.)

S – Support (Support your inference with facts from the text and your own experiences and knowledge.)

2. Use the KIS Strategy Examples transparency to practice the strategy with your students. Model each step in the first paragraph by thinking aloud. For example, I begin by saying:

I'll read the paragraph first. Then I'll go back and underline some key words. Let's see, I think new puppy, deep hole, accident, dad, yard work, would have noticed the hole, *and* filled it up *might be important words. I've raised several dogs, and I know that puppies love to dig holes in the ground. I also know that neither Joshua nor his father dug the hole. From those key words and my own experiences, I can infer that the puppy dug the hole.*

3. Slowly get students involved in the strategy. The table below shows how I gradually increase student participation in the process.

	Key Words	**Infer**	**Support**
Paragraph 1	teacher	teacher	teacher
Paragraph 2	teacher	students	teacher
Paragraph 3	students	teacher	students
Paragraph 4	students	students	students

4. When students feel comfortable with the strategy, let them practice it on their own. Distribute the Practicing the KIS Strategy reproducible. Quickly review the three steps in the strategy before the students begin to work independently. As they work, move around the room and prompt them with questions as necessary.

5. Then have partners compare one another's work. Again, emphasize that there will be a diversity of conclusions because of the background knowledge and experiences of each individual. Tell students NOT to change their answers because their partners have different ones.

6. Discuss the possible inferences for each paragraph with your entire class. Try to distill all the inferences into one that would apply well to the paragraph.

Closing the Lesson

Use one or more of these activities to wrap up the mini-lesson.

✱ **Writing:** Have students write two to three paragraphs. Instead of directly stating some information, they should use clues. (For example, FIRST PARAGRAPH: Select a place your readers will recognize. Provide clues, but do not directly identify the location. SECOND PARAGRAPH: Select an emotion for a particular character. Do not directly state why the character is experiencing the emotion.) Collect the paragraphs to use in the next lesson.

✱ **Auditory:** For this activity, use the completed Inferential Reflection Sheet from Mini-Lesson 1. Ask students to use the KIS strategy to explain the inferences they made about the location in Paragraph 3a. Then let volunteers read aloud the paragraphs they wrote. Can the rest of the students infer what the location or emotion is? How did the KIS strategy help them make their inferences?

Answers

KIS Strategy Examples, page 15 (Answers represent a reasonable inference.)

1. Inference: The new puppy dug the hole. Support: Many puppies love to dig; Joshua's dad keeps the lawn neat; neither Joshua nor his dad knew who dug the hole.

2. Inference: Someone else may have been scheduling appointments while Mary was out of the office. Support: She rarely makes scheduling mistakes; there were three mistakes in one week.

3. Inference: Emma wouldn't buy Super Duper Water Spray. Support: She is a person who doesn't like to waste money on new items. Water spray is something you don't have to buy.

Practicing the KIS Strategy, page 16 (Answers represent a reasonable inference.)

1. Inference: Lu and Seth are probably in New York City. Support: They're touring a big, busy city; the long elevator ride might be the one taken to reach the top of the Empire State Building.

2. Inference: Frankie probably heard people riding a roller coaster. Support: Terror and excitement in their voices could be their screams on the drops and turns of the ride; since they were heard from a long distance they may be high up in the air; the rattle of chains could be the sound of roller coaster cars climbing hills.

3. Inference: The setting is most likely a library. Support: The kids are hushed by adults; they are surrounded by reading materials; they can borrow books with a card.

KIS Strategy:
An Inference Strategy to Remember

K – Key words are underlined.

I – Infer. Predict what information is missing by thinking about the key words.

S – Support the inference by explaining why it is correct. Base your explanation on your own past experiences and knowledge.

Comprehension Mini-Lessons: Inference & Cause and Effect   Scholastic Teaching Resources

KIS Strategy Examples

Underline the key words in each paragraph. Then make an inference and support it.

Paragraph 1

Joshua went into the backyard to play on the swing set. His new puppy, Rascal, ran beside him. As Joshua was running toward the play area, he twisted his ankle. The accident caused him a lot of pain. Joshua's dad was always doing yard work and making sure that the grass was perfectly cut and the ground was even. Certainly, he would have noticed that hole and filled it up. Neither Joshua nor his father could figure out how that hole appeared. Who or what do you think caused the hole?

Inference: _____

_____

Support: _____

_____

_____

Paragraph 2

Mary has been a receptionist at Hair Clips for seven years. She rarely makes mistakes in scheduling customers. Last week, two hairdressers complained that three of their regular customers missed their appointments because of schedul-ing errors. What could have happened?

Inference: _____

_____

Support: _____

_____

_____

Paragraph 3

Emma is a very cautious shopper. She rarely takes risks, and she has a hard time buying new items unless she knows she won't waste her money. Emma sticks to her shopping list unless there's a sale, and she's been wanting to buy the item. You won't ever see Emma wasting her money. In fact, her family calls her the Tightwad Money Manager. Which of the following items would Emma most likely *not* buy: toothpaste, Super Duper Water Spray, beans, bubble gum?

Inference: _____

_____

Support: _____

_____

Practicing the KIS Strategy

Use the KIS strategy to make and support inferences.

1. What a long elevator ride it was! Lu and Seth couldn't wait to see the view through the wire fence. The wind was blowing through their hair as they looked down. The cars on the street looked like toy cars. What an amazing city this was!

Where were they?

Inference: _____

_____

Support: _____

_____

_____

2. Frankie could hear the people's screams from a long distance. She could hear terror and excitement in the screams. The sound of the screams occurred intermittently. A brief moment of silence would be followed by full-force screams. Frankie could also hear what she thought might be the rattle of chains.

What could be going on?

Inference: _____

_____

Support: _____

_____

_____

3. The kids were allowed to be here without their parents, but they were told to whisper three times by different adults. The place was big, cool, and quiet. Computers were set up by the information desk so people could find exactly what they needed or use the Internet for research. The kids looked at some magazines, listened to some CDs, read a few short books, and then saw a short puppet show. By using a special card, they were able to borrow some items.

What kind of place is this?

Inference: _____

_____

Support: _____

_____

_____

Comprehension Mini-Lessons: Inference & Cause and Effect Scholastic Teaching Resources

Ice Cream Inferences

Opening the Lesson

✽ To review the KIS strategy with my students, I use the inference-based paragraphs they wrote about a location and an emotion in Mini-Lesson 2.

✽ After randomly distributing the paragraphs (but making sure that no student receives his or her own work), I ask my students to employ the KIS strategy to make inferences about the two paragraphs and think about feedback to give to the authors.

✽ Then readers and authors pair off and discuss their inferences. Do the authors agree with the inferences? If not, the partners try to determine why their inferences are different. Were key words missed, or can key words be added to the paragraph? Did the author make assumptions about a reader's knowledge or experiences?

Teaching the Lesson

1. Explain to students that there are three steps in making a good inference.

    a. Locate facts in the text that will help you make an inference.

    b. Ask other people for their opinions or write down any opinion statements from the text.

    c. Figure out what you know and believe about the topic (your background knowledge, opinions, and experiences).

By considering these factors, they can make logical judgments about the missing information from the text (inferences).

2. Working with the Ice Cream Inferences reproducible and the fables will help students become familiar with the three steps. Distribute copies of the fables to your students. Then place the Ice Cream Inferences transparency on the overhead. Before you read aloud the first fable, "The Donkey and the Dog," remind students that a fable is a story that teaches a lesson.

3. Show students how information from the fable can be plotted on the Ice Cream Inferences transparency. Begin by summarizing the facts from the story. Then ask students for their opinions about the donkey and the dog. Model the background knowledge, opinions, and experiences that you bring, and how they inform your inference.

Objective

Students make inferences about fables by evaluating facts, opinions from others, and background knowledge.

Materials

Student paragraphs from Mini-Lesson 2

Reproducibles

Ice Cream Inferences, page 19 (Make 1 transparency and 1 double-sided copy for each student.)

Three Fables, page 20 (Make 1 copy for each student.)

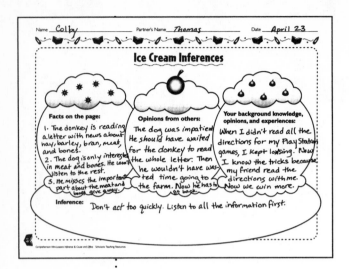

Name _Colby_   Partner's Name _Thomas_   Date _April 23_

Ice Cream Inferences

Facts on the page:
1. The donkey is reading a letter with news about hay, barley, bran, meat, and bones.
2. The dog is only interested in meat and bones. He won't listen to the rest.
3. He misses the important part about the meat and bones give away.

Opinions from others:
The dog was impatient. He should have waited for the donkey to read the whole letter. Then he wouldn't have wasted time going to the farm. Now he has to go back.

Your background knowledge, opinions, and experiences:
When I didn't read all the directions for my PlayStation games, I kept losing. Now I know the tricks because my friend read the directions with me. Now we win more.

Inference: Don't act too quickly. Listen to all the information first.

Comprehension Mini-Lessons: Inference & Cause and Effect Scholastic Teaching Resources

For instance, I might say:

"The dog seems selfish and impatient. He's only interested in what's important to him—meat and bones. One day, he might miss learning something really important because of his impatience. I can infer that the point of this fable is that it's important to be patient and enjoy what you read. Even if the information doesn't seem important to you at first, chances are that you'll learn something."

Remind students that the inference a reader makes at the end of a fable is the answer to the question, "What is this fable really teaching or saying?"

4. Now pair students and let them practice using this strategy. Hand out a double-sided copy of the Ice Cream Inferences reproducible to each student (they'll use the second side for the assessment activity below). Have partners read the next fable, "The Lion and the Hare" and write their individual responses on the Ice Cream Inferences reproducible. To fill out the "Opinions from others" section, tell students to ask their partners for their opinions. Although both partners will probably record the same facts, their opinions, background knowledge, and therefore, inferences may be different. Make sure students understand why their inferences may differ from those of their partner.

5. Discuss the fable with the class and compare responses.

Closing the Lesson

Use one or more of these activities to wrap up the mini-lesson.

* **Journal:** Challenge students to explain how each of the Ice Cream Inferences steps helps them create better inferences.

* **Assessment:** Have students read the final fable, "The Boar and the Fox" and complete the other side of their Ice Cream Inferences reproducible.

* **Verbal:** Have students use the fables and the Ice Cream Inferences graphic organizer to teach this strategy to a friend or a family member. You can make extra copies of the reproducible or students can draw the graphic organizer on notebook paper.

Answers
Three Fables, page 20: (Answers represent a reasonable inference; answers may vary.)
"The Donkey and the Dog": Take the time to read thoroughly. Even if the information doesn't seem interesting or important at first, you may need it later.
"The Lion and the Hare": In trying to get something better, you might lose the good thing you already had.
"The Boar and the Fox": Plan ahead. Procrastination could cost you dearly!

Ice Cream Inferences

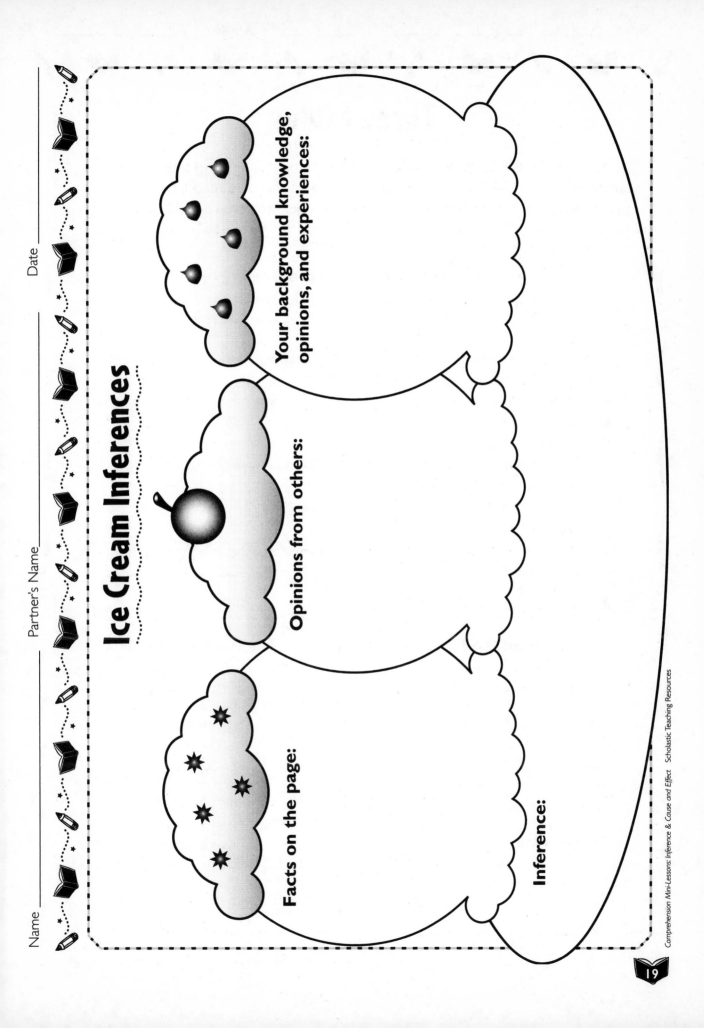

Facts on the page:

Opinions from others:

Your background knowledge, opinions, and experiences:

Inference:

Three Fables

Choose one of these fables and complete the Ice Cream Inferences page. Remember that fables teach us life lessons. Ask yourself: What is the fable teaching me? How can I apply its lesson to my life? Use your inference skills to come up with an answer.

The Donkey and the Dog

A donkey and a dog were traveling together when they saw a letter on the ground. The donkey began to read the letter to the dog. It concerned hay, barley, and bran, which the dog was not interested in.

He interrupted the donkey. "Who cares about hay, barley, and bran? Skip a few paragraphs, Donkey. You might find something interesting about meat and bones."

The donkey, who did love hay, barley, and bran, skimmed the letter. "You're right! Here's something about free bones."

The dog whirled in excitement. "Where? Where?"

"Be still, and let me finish reading the letter," the donkey answered. "It says that free bones will be given out at Shipley's Farm on—"

"I know where that is!" the dog said, and he ran down the road.

"Wait!" the donkey cried. "There's more!"

When the panting dog reached the farm, he found out that the bones were to be given out two days later.

The Lion and the Hare

A lion came upon a sleeping hare at the edge of a field. As he was about to devour the hare, he saw a deer leap by. The lion left the napping hare to chase the deer.

A moment later, the hare awoke and, quicker than a wink, ran away.

The lion continued to chase the deer. No matter how fast he ran, he couldn't catch it. Exhausted, the lion trudged back to the field to look for the hare. He discovered that it had escaped.

"Let this be a lesson," the lion sighed.

The Boar and the Fox

A boar was standing next to a tree, sharpening his tusks on the trunk. A fox stopped to watch. The boar was working so hard that the tree and nearby shrubs shook.

"Why are you sharpening your tusks?" asked the fox. "There aren't any hunters around."

"The answer is obvious," replied the boar. "If I were attacked, I certainly wouldn't have time to sharpen my tusks. But if I have them ready and sharp, I'll be able to put them to good use!"

Fables adapted from *Aesop's Fables* by Roberto Piumini (Barron's, 1989)

Comprehension Mini-Lessons: Inference & Cause and Effect Scholastic Teaching Resources

The Reasons Behind Our Answers

Opening the Lesson

❀ I begin this lesson by opening the following discussion: *Have you ever gotten irritated or mad at someone because his or her opinion was different from yours? Has anyone ever gotten angry with you because your opinion was different? Are such strong negative responses really logical? Can one person's opinion be better than someone else's? If you think so, can you give examples?*

❀ Throughout the discussion, I act as a guide rather than a leader. For example, if tempers start to flare, I jump in and ask my students how such strong responses make them feel and what they think is driving the responses. By the end of the discussion, they usually have a good sense of how much people's opinions can differ and the importance of respecting one another's opinions.

❀ I then emphasize that opinions—those values and beliefs we sometimes feel so strongly about—can impact the inferences we make when we read.

Teaching the Lesson

1. Distribute a copy of the story "The Planet Boom Boom" to each of your students. Tell students to follow along as you read aloud the story.

2. After the reading, have students decide whether they agree or disagree with each of the inference statements at the bottom of the page. They must also write a brief explanation as to why they agree or disagree next to the statement that includes their own opinion about it. Suggest that they underline key words or phrases from the passage that helped them form their opinions. Emphasize that there are no right or wrong answers, but that it is important that they provide reasons to support their opinions.

3. Read aloud each statement, and call on volunteers to share what they wrote. Explain that there isn't one right answer. Each person's reasons are based on his or her reading of the text and prior knowledge or life experiences.

4. The next activity will show students how they can come to different conclusions about the same thing. To model the activity, write the following quote (or one of your favorite quotes) on the chalkboard: *"We find comfort among those who agree with us—growth among those who don't."—Frank A. Clark*

Give students a few minutes to think about what the quote means. Then present your own

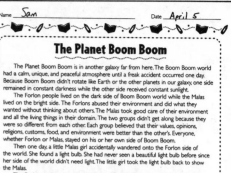

inference by thinking aloud. For instance, for the above quote, I say, *"I think this quote has a lot to say about what we've been discussing today. If everyone agrees with us or we agree with them, then our thinking doesn't stretch or change. But if someone has a different opinion than we do, it can help us think about an idea or a subject in new and different ways."*

5. Then distribute a Quote Reasoning reproducible to each student. Have them complete it independently.

6. When everyone has completed the task, divide your class into small groups to share their responses for each quote. This discussion should last about fifteen to twenty minutes.

Closing the Lesson

Use one or more of these activities to wrap up the mini-lesson.

* **Assessment:** Distribute the Reasoning Reflection reproducible, and have students complete it individually.

* **Students Working Together:** Compile a list of quotes from a book or an Internet Web site such as *http://www.quotationspage.com*. Let pairs or groups of students choose a quote and then collaborate on writing an inference about it. Set aside time for them to share their work with the entire class.

The Planet Boom Boom

The planet Boom Boom is in another galaxy far from here. The Boom Boom world had a calm, unique, and peaceful atmosphere until a freak accident occurred one day. Because Boom Boom didn't rotate like Earth or the other planets in our galaxy, one side remained in constant darkness while the other side received constant sunlight.

The Forlon people lived on the dark side of Boom Boom while the Malas lived on the bright side. The Forlons abused their environment and did what they wanted without thinking about others. The Malas took good care of their environment and all the living things in their domain. The two groups didn't get along because they were so different from each other. Each group believed that their values, opinions, religions, customs, food, and environment were better than the other's. Everyone, whether Forlon or Malas, stayed on his or her own side of Boom Boom.

Then one day, a little Malas girl accidentally wandered onto the Forlon side of the world. She found a lightbulb. She had never seen a beautiful lightbulb before since her side of the world didn't need light. The little girl took the lightbulb back to show the Malas.

The Forlons believed that she had stolen the lightbulb on purpose, and they attacked the Malas. They bombed Malas homes, lakes, trees, and other beautiful places. The Malas were not prepared for war. They had no way of retaliating because they had never dreamed that such a conflict would happen.

Read each statement. Decide whether you agree or disagree with it and circle your choice. Then, explain your choice and state your opinion.

1. The Forlons would make terrible neighbors. Agree/Disagree _____

_____

2. The Malas were better people than the Forlons. Agree/Disagree _____

_____

3. The Forlons were prepared. Agree/Disagree _____

_____

4. The Malas were not well organized. Agree/Disagree _____

_____

5. It would be difficult for the Forlons to live on planet Earth. Agree/Disagree

_____

6. It would be difficult for the Malas to live on planet Earth. Agree/Disagree

_____

Comprehension Mini-Lessons: Inference & Cause and Effect   Scholastic Teaching Resources

Quote Reasoning

What does each quote mean? Write your inference (the meaning you get from the quote) and supporting reasons. (Remember: Your opinions and experiences affect the inferences you make!)

1. "I find the harder I work, the more luck I seem to have."—Thomas Jefferson

Inference: _____

_____

Reasons for my inference: _____

_____

2. "The best way to predict the future is to invent it."—Alan Kay

Inference: _____

_____

Reasons for my inference: _____

_____

3. "He who asks is a fool for five minutes, but he who doesn't ask remains a fool forever." —Chinese proverb

Inference: _____

_____

Reasons for my inference: _____

_____

4. "No one can make you feel inferior without your consent."—Eleanor Roosevelt

Inference: _____

_____

Reasons for my inference: _____

_____

Comprehension Mini-Lessons: Inference & Cause and Effect   Scholastic Teaching Resources

Reasoning Reflection Sheet

1. Did all the members of your group agree on the meaning of each quote? How different were the answers and reasons?

_____

_____

_____

_____

_____

2. Do you think your reasons and inferences were better than those of the other group members? Explain why you think this.

_____

_____

_____

_____

_____

3. What has this activity taught you about respecting other people's opinions?

_____

_____

_____

_____

_____

4. Why is it important to have reasons to support your inferences?

_____

_____

_____

_____

_____

Comprehension Mini-Lessons: Inference & Cause and Effect   Scholastic Teaching Resources

Test-Taking Format

Opening the Lesson

✤ I open this lesson by asking my students if they've heard the phrase "reading between the lines." To generate discussion about the phrase, I ask: *How can you read between the lines of a book? What do you think that phrase means?*

✤ When my students realize that the phrase describes making an inference, I display the Reading Between the Lines transparency on the overhead. (Cover all the text below the top paragraph.) Then I read aloud the paragraph, or ask a volunteer to do so.

✤ After uncovering the questions, I let volunteers answer them. I read aloud each question and wait for their responses. In this activity, I'm looking for more than a "yes" or "no" answer. I want my students to describe how they arrived at their answers.

✤ Finally I reveal the detailed paragraph at the bottom of the transparency and ask how it differs from the first paragraph. Students are usually amazed at what they were able to infer from the paragraph that had fewer words. I emphasize this point: *Authors often expect their readers to read between the lines. They expect you to make inferences as you read.*

Teaching the Lesson

1. Ask students to think about some of the assessment tests they've taken. Do they remember questions that asked them to make inferences about a paragraph or a passage? Explain that any reading or language arts standardized test will contain questions that will require them to infer information about a piece of writing.

2. Explain to students that there are strategies they can use that will help them answer inference questions in testing situations. Share the following steps with them:

   • If you can't find the answer to the question in the text, you know you must "read between the lines" or infer the information based on the text. Questions might have the key words *tell*, *know*, or *why*; for example, "How can you tell . . ." "What do you know

about . . ." or "You can tell from this paragraph that . . ."

- By process of elimination, you can get rid of answers that don't fit logically into the passage. Only one of the answers should make sense if you inserted it into the passage.

- Place a checkmark in the passage where the missing information (your answer choice) could be placed to make a smooth, logical paragraph. This is one way to make sure that you have chosen the correct answer.

3. Practice the strategies with your students. Distribute the Inference Paragraph Practice page to each student. Also place a copy on the overhead. Read aloud the first paragraph, and then have students answer the questions independently. Model your response to the first question, for example, *I think Rosario is a teacher. In the second sentence she talks about grading papers.* Then call on volunteers to share their answers. Ask how they arrived at the answers and where the answers might be included in the paragraph. Place a checkmark in the paragraph.

4. Now have students create four multiple-choice responses for each question in the first paragraph. This will give you the opportunity to show them how some answer choices can be tricky. Supply these answer choices for the second question: A. California, B. New York City, C. on a farm, and D. in a small town. Although California is mentioned in the paragraph, it would probably *not* be the best answer. People usually vacation in places where they don't live. Point out that B is the best choice. Having students create answer choices will give them a greater awareness of the testing format.

5. Then have pairs of students work together to write answer choices for the questions for the second paragraph. Guide their practice as necessary. They should write their choices on a separate sheet of paper, sign their names, and turn it in to you.

Closing the Lesson

Use one or more of these activities to wrap up the mini-lesson.

* **Assessment:** Have students complete the Inference Passage Practice independently.

* **Journal:** Pose these questions for students to write about in their journals: How did this mini-lesson affect your understanding of making inferences? Do you think it strengthened your ability to answer inference questions on tests?

Answers
Inference Passage Practice, page 30: 1. B; 2. A

Reading Between the Lines

The Cat in the Garage

The cat jumped out of the truck and onto the hot pavement. It leaped and hopped past LeAnn and into her cool garage. LeAnn looked at her watch, sighed, and began to look around, calling, "Kitty! Kitty!" The cat scooted underneath her car. If only the cat knew that LeAnn was trying to help it!

1. Does LeAnn like cats?

2. Is LeAnn a busy person?

3. What does LeAnn want to do for the cat?

4. Is the cat afraid?

5. Will the cat stay in LeAnn's garage?

Paragraph with inferences included:

The Cat in the Garage

The Furniture Fair truck arrived and opened its back door to deliver LeAnn's furniture. A cat jumped out of the truck and onto the hot pavement. It leaped and hopped into LeAnn's cool garage. LeAnn loved dogs, but she would rather not own a cat. Now she had to spend her time looking for a cat she had never seen before. She had too many things to do to spend the day looking for a cat. LeAnn looked at her watch, sighed, and began to look around, calling, "Kitty! Kitty!" The cat scooted underneath her car. If the cat only knew that LeAnn was trying to help it! She wanted to take it back to its owner, or at least find a home for it. Eventually the cat came out, and LeAnn was able to find its owner.

Comprehension Mini-Lessons: Inference & Cause and Effect   Scholastic Teaching Resources

Inference Paragraph Practice

Read each paragraph. Then choose the best answer.

An Ocean Scare

Rosario was enjoying her vacation in the California sun. She was lying on a raft in the ocean. This was perfect, Rosario thought. There was no noise—no children screaming, no horns honking—and there were no papers to grade. All she could hear was the crashing of the waves onto the beach. Rosario sighed and looked around her at the beauty of the ocean. Then she saw something long and gray coming toward her on an approaching wave. She thought, "This could only be one thing!" and started yelling for help. She paddled back to shore as quickly as she could. She made it to the shore in one piece, but she realized that many people were laughing at her.

1. What do you think Rosario's job is? _____

2. Where do you think Rosario lives? _____

3. What do you think Rosario saw in the ocean? _____

4. Was Rosario scared? _____

5. Why do you think people were laughing at Rosario? _____

_____

Who Cooks the Fish?

Bob and Darius went fishing in Bennet Springs, Illinois. Each man caught a fish—the biggest fish he had ever caught. They couldn't wait to show their wives, who had decided to go hiking instead of fishing. They talked about how the same fish had taken two to three flies off their poles. They felt like they had taught those fish a lesson by catching them. They handed their fish to their wives and walked to the fire, still talking. The women put the fish on the ground and their fists on their hips.

1. Were Bob and Darius proud of their fish? _____

2. How do you think the wives felt about the fish and their husbands? _____

_____

3. Why do you think they felt this way? _____

4. Why were Bob and Darius walking toward the fire? _____

5. Do you think Bob and Darius fish often? _____

Inference Passage Practice

Read each passage. Then choose the best answer.

Animal Communication

Animals can't speak in words, but they have many other ways to "talk" to each other. Here's a look at how some creatures communicate in the wild.

Giant otters speak in a unique language of whistles, whines, squeals, and snorts. Each sound has a different meaning. One type of snort warns other otters of danger, such as when a predator is nearby.

Red howler monkeys communicate by howling. Their howls can be heard up to three miles away. In fact, these monkeys are the world's noisiest land animals.

Wolves curl their lips above their teeth and snarl at other wolves to show who's in charge, and to warn other wolves to back off. Wolves will also howl to signal danger.

The elephant seal uses its amazing inflatable nose and its nostrils as a giant microphone.

1. The passage would probably go on to discuss—

(A) what red howler monkeys eat.

(B) how other animals communicate.

(C) where giant otters live.

(D) how wolves talk to giant otters.

Trick-or-Treating for UNICEF

Ghosts and ghouls have raised more than $100 million to help poor children around the world. How have they done this? By trick-or-treating for UNICEF, the United Nations' Children's Fund.

Founded in 1946, UNICEF has helped children in more than 140 poor or war-torn countries receive food, shelter, and medicine. Every year it adopts a new slogan, such as "Increase the Peace."

A group of kids from Philadelphia founded the trick-or-treat for UNICEF program in 1950. They raised seventeen dollars. Since then, kids dressed in their Halloween best have followed suit—and, as the program has grown, the amount of money has grown far beyond seventeen dollars. In a recent year, kids helped raised $2.1 million! This year, they could raise even more.

1. From this article, you could guess that—

(A) a large number of children participate in trick-or-treat for UNICEF.

(B) kids from Philadelphia are more concerned than other kids.

(C) the trick-or-treat for UNICEF program made more in the 1950s than it does now.

(D) children receive more candy when they trick-or-treat for UNICEF.

Comprehension Mini-Lessons: Inference & Cause and Effect Scholastic Teaching Resources

Putting It All Together: Igniting Idioms Game

Preparing for the Project

✿ Since my students will be creating their own board games, I bring in a variety of games for them to examine. I also make a transparency of the sample game board on page 34 and sample game cards.

✿ I have copies of short mystery stories available. These will serve as models for the mysteries students will write for the game.

Introducing the Project

1. To introduce idioms to your class, act grumpy and use this idiomatic expression: *I got up on the wrong side of the bed this morning.* Ask students: *Do you really think a bed has a wrong and a right side? Or is this a figure of speech—does it mean something else?*

2. Tell students that this figure of speech is called an idiom, and that idioms appear in every language. Then have them think of other idioms they've heard. Challenge students to make a connection between idioms and inferences. (You have to read between the lines to determine their meanings.)

3. Explain that they will be creating a game based on idioms and inference mini-stories. Distribute the Student Project Sheet, and go over it. After pairing students, hand out the rubrics so they can see how they will be graded—and how they will grade others!

Assessing the Project

✿ Let pairs play each other's games. Have them complete the Idiom Game Rubric to evaluate the game and give their peers feedback. You should also use the rubric to grade the game.

✿ Have students fill out the Idiom Reflection Sheet.

Objective

Students relate idioms to making inferences by creating a board game.

Duration

two to three days

Materials

Scholastic Dictionary of Idioms by Marvin Terban (Scholastic, 1996); *Two-Minute Mysteries* by Donald J. Sobol (Scott Foresman, 1991) or other mini-mysteries; for each pair of students: poster-board, markers, and crayons, rulers, paper, 20 3" x 5") index cards, dice, plastic bag, objects to use as game tokens; a variety of board games (optional), container

Reproducibles

Student Project Sheet, pages 32–33 (Make 1 copy for each student.)

Sample Game Board, page 34 (Make 1 copy for each pair; make 1 transparency [optional].)

Idiom Game Rubric, page 35 (Make 1 copy for each pair.)

Idiom Reflection Sheet, page 36 (Make 1 copy for each student.)

Putting It All Together Inference Project

Igniting Idioms Game

Follow these steps to create your own idiom game. You'll make a game board, game cards, and answer key.

1. Make the idiom game cards.

❋ Use index cards to make at least 16 idiom game cards. Write IDIOM on the front of each card and number it. A sample card is shown. A good definition of this idiom would be "to remain calm."

❋ Refer to the *Scholastic Dictionary of Idioms* to write your idioms. On the back of each card write an idiom, a sentence containing the idiom, and how many spaces the player can move.

2. Make the whodunit game cards.

❋ Each partner writes two mini-mystery stories. Use separate sheets of paper. BE SURE TO GIVE CLUES TO THE SOLUTION, BUT DON'T GIVE AWAY THE SOLUTION TO THE MYSTERY. Let your reader infer what happens!

❋ Make a whodunit game card for each story using an index card. Write WHODUNIT on the front of the card, and number it. Indicate on the back of the card how many spaces the player should move if he or she is successful in guessing whodunit.

❋ When a player draws a whodunit card, he or she reads aloud the story and tries to solve the mystery.

IDIOM #1

Idiom: Keep your shirt on.
Sentence containing idiom: I was in such a hurry to leave that my mom told me to keep my shirt on.
What does the idiom mean? Tell the other players.
If the answer is correct, move forward 2 spaces.

WHODUNIT #1

If you guessed whodunit correctly, move forward 4 spaces.

Mini-Mystery for WHODUNIT Card 1
"Who Stole the Sweater?" by Kristen H.

Heather and Chelcie were two fourteen-year-old girls getting ready for their first year in high school. They decided it was time to get some new clothes for this new school year. They went to the mall and headed for their favorite store, Express. As they looked around, they realized that everything was much too expensive for them. Right then was when they ran into their good friend, Amber.

Amber told the girls that Weathervane (their second favorite store) was having a huge sale. The three girls walked into the store and began searching for the perfect outfit. All of a sudden, Amber ran into a table and all kinds of sweaters fell all over the floor. She began picking up her mess, but fell in love with a pink cotton sweater. She wanted it so badly, but still cleaned up all the other sweaters. When Heather and Chelcie saw she was finished, they met her at the cash register to buy what they had found. After the items were bought, Amber asked Heather if she could look in the bag to see her new clothes. When she was done, she handed it back to Heather, and they began to leave the store.

Then, Chelcie saw another item on a rack and said, "Hey, wait! I need to check this out!" After looking at the sweaters for her size, she concluded that her size was all gone. "Oh well, I'll just have to keep shopping until I find a sweater similar to that one. Let's go girls!"

As they were walking out of the Weathervane store, the alarms went off and the girls were searched all over for any stolen items. In Heather's bag a pink-cotton sweater was found, and she denied everything she had been accused of. So the question is who stole the sweater?

Comprehension Mini-Lessons: Inference & Cause and Effect Scholastic Teaching Resources

3. Make the Game Board.

✿ Think of a name for your game. Write it on the posterboard (your game board).

✿ Include the following spaces on the board:

• a Start space and a Goal space

• at least 6 fun spaces (lose a turn, go back ___ spaces, shortcut, free turn, and so on)

• 16 idiom and 2 whodunit spaces When a player lands on these spaces, he or she draws a card.

✿ Decide what objects to use as game pieces.

4. Create the answer key.

✿ Write an answer key for the idiom meanings and the whodunit solutions on a separate sheet of paper.

5. Create the game directions.

✿ Write out step-by-step directions for playing your game. Have fun and be creative—but be clear!

✿ After writing out your directions, use them to play a sample game. You may find that you need to revise them.

6. Play and grade another pair's game.

✿ Write your names on a scrap of paper. Fold it and drop it in the container on the teacher's desk.

✿ Draw a name from the container to find out whose game you will play.

✿ As you play, use the Idiom Game Rubric to grade the game. Turn in your completed rubric to your teacher. (Your teacher will grade your game, too, so you'll receive two grades!)

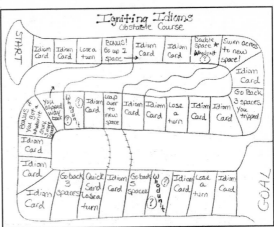

ANSWER KEY

Idiom Card #1—to remain calm   **Idiom Card #2**—to get angry

Whodunit Card 1: When Amber knocked over the sweaters, she put every one of them back, except the one she desperately wanted. When she looked inside Heather's bag, she stuffed the sweater in it and handed it back to Heather. Amber got caught when Heather denied having taken it, and she was questioned. The mall security guard called Amber's mother and talked to her about what happened. She had quite a consequence to handle.

Igniting Idioms Game Directions

GOAL: To get to the finish line first

Roll die when it's your turn. If you land on a space called IDIOM or WHODUNIT, you will need to pull a card from the pile and try to guess the meaning of the idiom OR tell whodunit. You must read it aloud so all members can hear it. Another member within your group will look in the answer key to see if your answer is correct.

If correct, move up the number of spaces the card tells you to. It's now the next person's turn.
If incorrect, you must move back the number of spaces written on the card. It will be the next person's turn.

Name(s) _____   Date _____

Idiom Game Rubric

Game creators: _____

CRITERIA	Incomplete 0	Okay 1	Good 2	WOW! 3	Score
The Cards 1. The cards are filled out correctly, contain good clues within sentences, and are neatly written.					
Whodunit Stories 2. The stories are good stories (not too easy and not too hard) that are unique.					
3. Each has an introduction, problem, and conclusion, and describes the characters well.					
4. Each contains important details.					
5. Each has correct grammar, spelling, punctuation, and capitalization.					
Game Board 6. The game board includes at least 24 spaces and has a title.					
7. It is colorful, creative, and neat.					
Directions and Answer Key 8. The directions and answer key are clear and easy to understand, and are neat.					

OUR COMMENTS:
I/We liked the following things about your game:

Here are some suggestions:

TOTAL SCORE: _____ /24

START

GOAL

Comprehension Mini-Lessons: Inference & Cause and Effect Scholastic Teaching Resources

Name(s) _____   Date _____

Idiom Game Rubric

Game creators: _____

CRITERIA	Incomplete 0	Okay 1	Good 2	WOW! 3	Score

The Cards

1. The cards are filled out correctly, contain good clues within sentences, and are neatly written.

Whodunit Stories

2. The stories are good stories (not too easy and not too hard) that are unique.

3. Each has an introduction, problem, and conclusion, and describes the characters well.

4. Each contains important details.

5. Each has correct grammar, spelling, punctuation, and capitalization.

Game Board

6. The game board includes at least 24 spaces and has a title.

7. It is colorful, creative, and neat.

Directions and Answer Key

8. The directions and answer key are clear and easy to understand, and are neat.

OUR COMMENTS:

I/We liked the following things about your game:

Here are some suggestions:

TOTAL SCORE: _____ /24

Idiom Reflection Sheet

1. What is an idiom?

_____

_____

_____

2. Tell why explaining an idiom is a great example of making an inference.

_____

_____

_____

_____

3. Give three examples of your favorite idioms and explain their inferred meanings.

_____

_____

_____

_____

_____

_____

_____

_____

4. Explain whether or not you enjoyed creating your idiom game.

_____

_____

_____

_____

Comprehension Mini-Lessons: Inference & Cause and Effect   Scholastic Teaching Resources

Cause and Effect

The Relationship Between Cause and Effect

Opening the Lesson

Objective

Students define cause and effect and organize relationships on a T-chart.

Materials

If You Give A Pig A Pancake by Laura Numeroff (HarperCollins, 1998) or a similar book; four or more blank transparencies (optional)

Reproducibles

T-Charts: Causes and Effects, page 40 (Make 1 copy for each student.)

✤ I like to read aloud a book filled with cause-and-effect relationships, such as *If You Give a Pig a Pancake*. After the reading, I ask my students to talk about how one event led to another in the story, and to give specific examples. You may prompt discussion by introducing the initial event: *"It all started when a girl gave a pig a pancake."*

✤ Then I expand the discussion of cause and effect by asking my students if they've ever experienced the kind of day the girl in the book had. Here's a prompt I use to get the discussion rolling: *"I was driving to work and had a flat tire. When I got out of the car to look at the tire, I fell into the mud and ruined my shoes and clothes. I decided to use my cell phone to call for help . . ."* This kind of story can go on and on, and it's okay if students begin to exaggerate the spiraling events in their stories. This can help them, and everyone else, make the connection between cause and effect.

✤ Finally I point out that all the stories are full of causes and effects: *"One event causes another event to happen and that keeps the story line or plot moving along. The effect tells what happens. The cause tells why it happened. Sometimes the effect becomes the cause of the next event, as in the story we read."*

Teaching the Lesson

1. Explain to students that they can keep track of simple causes and effects by creating a T-chart. Draw the following T-chart on the chalkboard or on a transparency.

EVENT: no paper in the classroom	
Cause	**Effect**
Students didn't bring paper to class.	They couldn't do writing assignments.
Someone took all the paper.	Students had to borrow paper from another class.
Teacher accidentally threw it away.	Students couldn't take math test.

Challenge students to contribute more causes and effects to the T-chart.

2. Now have students use a T-chart to create their own cause-and-effect scenarios for a noisy classroom and/or being tardy.

3. Change the T-chart to expand the concept of the relationships between cause and effect. In this T-chart, students will supply an effect for a cause, or a cause for an effect.

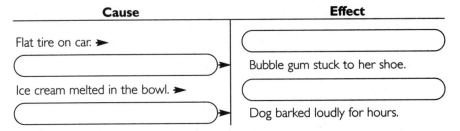

Cause	Effect
Flat tire on car. ➤	( )
( ) ➤	Bubble gum stuck to her shoe.
Ice cream melted in the bowl. ➤	( )
( ) ➤	Dog barked loudly for hours.

Remind students to constantly ask themselves whether one event caused another event *or* what the effect of an event was. Share this strategy for determining cause and effect with them: *"Check your answers by reading the statements as: (blank) caused (blank) to happen. Fill in the first blank with the cause, and fill in the second blank with the effect."*

4. Now let students create their own T-charts with three cause-and-effect pairs that mirror the last example. They should exchange charts and fill in the incomplete causes and effects.

Closing the Lesson

Use one or more of these activities to wrap up the mini-lesson.

✱ **Assessment:** Have students work independently to complete the T-Charts: Causes and Effects reproducible.

✱ **Students Working Together:** Have each student create T-charts with three unrelated causes and effects. Direct them to exchange charts with partners. Each partner supplies the missing effects and causes. This activity always produces some funny results. Be sure to allow time for partners to share their work with the rest of the class. There will be some funny ones!

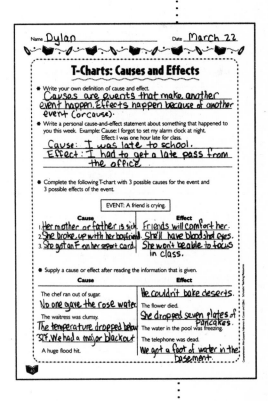

T-Charts: Causes and Effects

✱ Write your own definition of cause and effect.

_____

_____

✱ Write a personal cause-and-effect statement about something that happened to you this week. Example: Cause: I forgot to set my alarm clock at night.
                    Effect: I was one hour late for class.

_____

_____

_____

✱ Complete the following T-chart with three possible causes for the event and three possible effects of the event.

EVENT: A friend is crying.

Cause	Effect
1. _____	_____
2. _____	_____
3. _____	_____

✱ Supply a cause or effect after reading the information that is given.

Cause	Effect
The chef ran out of sugar.	_____
_____	The flower died.
The waitress was clumsy.	_____
_____	The water in the pool was freezing.
_____	The telephone was dead.
A huge flood hit.	_____

Comprehension Mini-Lessons: Inference & Cause and Effect   Scholastic Teaching Resources

Graphing Cause-and-Effect Relationships

Opening the Lesson

❀ I open the lesson by having my students play a quick game of Cause-and-Effect Charades. Cut out the Charade Cards on page 44, and place them in a container. Each card contains a cause and a related effect. (You may want to add some of your own cause-and-effect examples.) Direct pairs of students to draw one card.

❀ To play the game, pairs act out the action described on the card: one student pantomimes the cause, then the other student acts out the effect. After pairs have finished their performance, the rest of the students try to guess the cause and the effect. I usually allot about one to two minutes for my students to guess the answer. (NOTE: Be flexible in accepting your students' guesses—take answers that are close to the original intent.)

Teaching the Lesson

1. Point out that by playing charades, students saw examples of how one cause can produce one effect. Some of the causes could generate many different effects. Share this example: *If you don't study for a test, the following effects might occur: you might toss and turn the night before the test; you might flunk the test; you might take the test and realize you knew more than you thought you did.* (Use with Cause-and-Effect Graphic Organizer 1, Multiple Effects, in step 2.)

Objective

Students use five different graphic organizers to explore cause-and-effect relationships.

Materials

container, scissors, paper and pens; posterboard, markers (optional)

Reproducibles

Charade Cards, page 44 (Make 1 copy.)

Cause-and-Effect Graphic Organizers 1–2, page 45 (Make 1 transparency.)

Cause-and-Effect Graphic Organizers 3–5, page 46 (Make 1 transparency.)

Graphing Cause and Effect, page 47 (Make 1 copy for each student.)

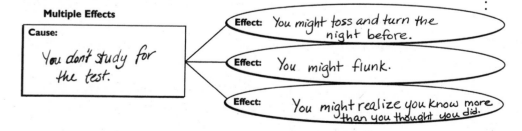

Multiple Effects

Cause: You don't study for the test.

Effect: You might toss and turn the night before.

Effect: You might flunk.

Effect: You might realize you know more than you thought you did.

Some effects have several causes. Present this example: *A child might come home from camp early because the following events happened: she broke her leg on a hike, she hated the camp, and she was allergic to many of the plants around the camp.* (Use with Cause-and-Effect Graphic Organizer 2, Multiple Causes, in step 2.)

Multiple Causes

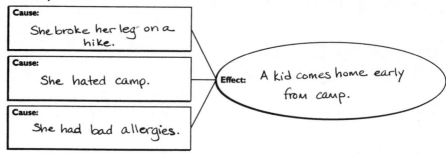

Tip . . . .

To illustrate a good use for the Cycle graphic organizer, tap into your science curriculum. Use one of the following natural cycles: water, rock, nitrogen, or carbon dioxide.

Some causes and effects are like a chain reaction—one event causes another event to occur, which causes another event to occur, and so on and so on. Use this example: *In the book* If You Give a Pig A Pancake, *the pig got a pancake, then she wanted syrup for it. Then the syrup made the pig sticky, which made her want a bath, and so on.* (Use with Cause-and-Effect Graphic Organizer 3, Chain Reaction, in step 2.)

Chain Reaction

Cause	Cause/Effect	Cause/Effect	Cause/Effect	Cause/Effect
The pig gets a pancake.	She wants syrup.	The syrup makes her sticky.	She decides to take a bath.	She wants bubbles in her bath.

2. So far, you've introduced scenarios that students can graph on three of the cause-and-effect graphic organizers. Display the graphic organizers on the overhead. (NOTE: You may also want to create posters of the five graphic organizers to hang in the classroom.) Read aloud the above examples again, and after each example, ask students to guess which graphic organizer goes with that example. You may want to fill in the organizers with students' suggestions. Also, find out which graphic organizer they think they would use to graph the game of charades they played (graphic organizer 4, Traditional).

Traditional

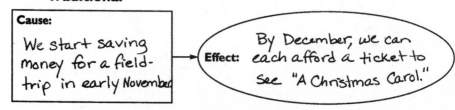

3. Direct your students' attention to the Chain Reaction graphic organizer. Be sure they understand why all the boxes after the first box say Cause/Effect. Since it is a chain reaction, an effect becomes a cause.

Also remind students that there may be more or fewer effects than indicated on the Multiple Effects, the Multiple Causes, and the Chain Reaction graphic organizers. They may add or delete boxes to make their information fit in the graphic organizer.

4. Set aside time for pairs of students to create their own examples for each type of graphic organizer (NOTE: Since the use of the Cycle graphic organizer is fairly limited, you might assign the topic or invite students do this one for extra credit).

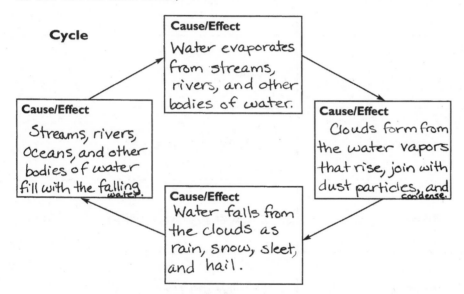

Cycle

Cause/Effect
Water evaporates from streams, rivers, and other bodies of water.

Cause/Effect
Clouds form from the water vapors that rise, join with dust particles, and condense.

Cause/Effect
Water falls from the clouds as rain, snow, sleet, and hail.

Cause/Effect
Streams, rivers, Oceans, and other bodies of water fill with the falling water.

Partners can draw and label the graphic organizers on separate sheets of paper and then complete them. Have partners share their favorite examples. Try to include a variety of examples for each graphic organizer.

Closing the Lesson

✤ **Assessment:** Have plenty of copies of the cause-and-effect graphic organizers on hand. Now that students have practiced using the graphic organizers, it's time to see if they can pick the best one to display the causes and effects in a passage. Challenge them to select and draw the organizer and complete the Graphing Cause and Effect reproducible independently.

Answers

Graphing Cause and Effect, page 47
"The Bombs That Ended the War" —Multiple Effects organizer; "The Civil War"—Multiple Causes organizer; "The Nitrogen Cycle"—Cycle organizer; "Micah's Rotten Day"—Chain Reaction organizer.

Charade Cards

Cut out the cards. Fold and place in a container for pairs of students to draw.
C = Cause, E = Effect

fold

C: Don't study for a test	E: Get nervous and anxious
C: Don't brush teeth at night	E: Get bad breath
C: Play with matches	E: Burn finger
C: Don't look before crossing street	E: Make cars swerve
C: Send flowers to someone	E: Make someone happy
C: Walk barefoot in the grass	E: Enjoy the cool sensation
C: Forget to wear your glasses	E: Run into furniture
C: Leave out food at the picnic	E: Ants eat the food
C: Eat too much food, too fast	E: Get a stomachache
C: Park in a no-parking zone	E: Get car towed

Comprehension Mini-Lessons: Inference & Cause and Effect Scholastic Teaching Resources

Cause-and-Effect Graphic Organizers 1–2

1. Multiple Effects

Cause:

Effect:

Effect:

Effect:

2. Multiple Causes

Cause:

Cause:

Cause:

Effect:

Comprehension Mini-Lessons: Inference & Cause and Effect   Scholastic Teaching Resources

Cause-and-Effect Graphic Organizers 3–5

3. Chain Reaction

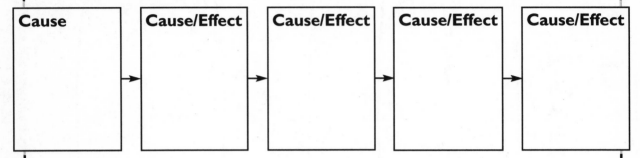

| Cause | | Cause/Effect | | Cause/Effect | | Cause/Effect | | Cause/Effect |

4. Traditional

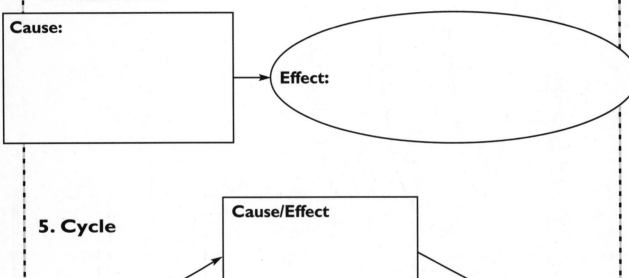

Cause:

Effect:

5. Cycle

Cause/Effect

Cause/Effect

Cause/Effect

Cause/Effect

Cause/Effect

Comprehension Mini-Lessons: Inference & Cause and Effect   Scholastic Teaching Resources

Graphing Cause and Effect

Read each paragraph. Then select one or two graphic organizers to graph the causes and effects in the paragraph. Draw the graphic organizers on separate sheets of paper and label them. Remember: You may need to add more boxes or ovals—or you may not use some of them.

The Bombs That Ended the War

On August 6, 1944, an atomic bomb was dropped on Hiroshima, Japan. The United States made this decision in order to end World War II. It was a long war. America entered the war on December 7, 1941, when Japan bombed Pearl Harbor, Hawaii. The atomic bomb immediately killed 100,000 people, and another 100,000 died from the aftereffects. The dropping of a second atomic bomb on Nagasaki three days later forced Japan to surrender. Today, a large number of Japanese citizens suffer from cancer because of the radiation from the bomb.

The Civil War (1861–1865)

The Civil War was fought between the northern and southern states in America. Several events caused the war. First of all, many Southerners owned slaves. The northern states wanted to abolish, or end, slavery. The South wanted to secede, to become independent, from the North and become a separate country. Harriet Beecher Stowe, the author of *Uncle Tom's Cabin*, taught many northern people what slavery was like in the South. Her book caused even more Northerners to want to end slavery.

The Nitrogen Cycle

Nitrogen is a gas that makes up about 78 percent of Earth's atmosphere. Nitrogen is very important for our Earth. Bacteria remove nitrogen from the air and add it to the soil. Plants use the nitrogen. Then animals take it in by eating the plants. When plants and animals die, nitrogen is released and returned to the air. Then the cycle starts over again when bacteria remove the nitrogen from the air.

Micah's Rotten Day

What a day! It all started when I got out of bed and slipped on the marbles I left on the floor. I fell flat on my face and twisted my right arm. It was quite painful to get up and go eat breakfast. I spilled a whole pitcher of orange juice when my arm gave out on me. My mom helped me clean up the mess and then rushed me off to school. Unfortunately, orange juice was still all over my clothes, which attracted ants when I sat on the ground at recess. The ants bit me about twenty times, and I had to go to the nurse's office. Even though I tried to explain what happened, she thought I was coming down with chicken pox and called my mother. When Mom picked me up, she took me straight to the doctor's office. Dr. Garza realized that the bumps were bites, but they were starting to swell. So she gave me a shot to decrease my allergic reaction to the ant bites. At home, I took a long nap. But first, I picked up every marble on the floor.

Comprehension Mini-Lessons: Inference & Cause and Effect Scholastic Teaching Resources

Ripple Effect Graphic Organizer

Opening the Lesson

Objective

Students understand that one event can lead to multiple causes and effects by using a graphic organizer to map out a current event.

Materials

information resources

Reproducibles

The Ripple Effect, page 50 (Make 2 transparencies. Make 1 copy for each student.)

✤ To begin this lesson, I explain that one event can often cause several other events to happen. These events, in turn, can cause even more events to happen and so on. The effects become causes that create other effects. A ripple of ideas occurs. I point out that this often happens in world events.

✤ Then I write a timely world topic on the chalkboard, such as "an increase in gasoline prices." I ask my students to brainstorm the possible effects of the increased price and write their responses as a list on the chalkboard.

✤ Since it's difficult to see the relationships among the listed causes and effects, I tell my students that I'm going to show them a graphic organizer that will link the causes and effects together.

Teaching the Lesson

1. Display the Ripple Effect transparency on the overhead. Model how to graph your students' responses to the topic of increased gas prices. You might explain it like this:

I start with the center space. I write the topic or problem there, which is an increase in gasoline prices. Then I move to the ring of stars that radiate from the center star. In these four stars, I write the events caused by our topic:

1. People will travel less.

2. Business transportation costs will increase.

3. A greater percentage of families' incomes will go toward fuel.

4. People will buy more gas-efficient vehicles.

Now, that's not where the issue ends. Just think what effects these events might cause! I'll write them in the next level of stars that ripple out from the first group of stars. I see that each of these second-tier stars has two more stars radiating out of it. Let's see, if people travel less, then their phone bills may be higher because they talk to their friends and relatives who live far away instead of visiting them. I'll write, "higher phone bills." And since people are traveling less, places won't earn as much money from tourists. I'll write, "less tourist revenue." I can see that I may not fill in every star at this level. I can also see that I could keep adding more and more stars because each effect becomes a cause that will have its own effects.

2. By analyzing world trends, we usually can see a ripple effect. Explain that a trend is a pattern of cause-and-effect behaviors that occurs over time. It usually moves in one direction—up to indicate growth or down to show a decline. Trends can be either short term or long term. Here are some examples of trends:

• More people are moving from the northern to the southern part of the U.S.

• An increasing number of people are shopping online instead of going into stores.

Discuss one of these trends with your students. Graph your discussion on a blank Ripple Effect transparency.

3. Then have pairs of students research the most current trends in topics such as the following:

pollution	population	weather	business
government	environment	families	food/nutrition
homelessness	energy	genetic engineering	science

Their research might come from current magazines, journals, Web sites, newspapers, books, and so on. They are welcome to ask an adult for help as well. As they research, students should be taking notes on the problems, their causes, and outcomes. They will use this information to complete a Ripple Effect graphic organizer. Remind them they may add additional stars—or that they may not fill up all of the outer-level stars.

Closing the Lesson

Use one or more of these activities to wrap up the mini-lesson.

✱ **Journal:** Here are some questions that each partner should answer after the Ripple Effect graphic organizer is done.

1. Why is the topic you chose important to think about?
2. Why did this topic interest you?
3. List the effects that are positive, and explain why.
4. List the effects that are negative, and explain why.
5. List any other causes that some of the effects could have had.
6. Do you think your graphic organizer will continue to expand? Explain your reasoning.

✱ **Verbal:** Have partners share their graphic organizers with the entire class. They should explain how one event led to several different effects, which led to even more effects.

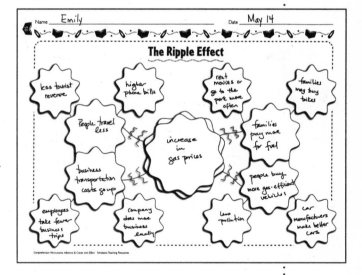

The Ripple Effect

Comprehension Mini-Lessons: Inference & Cause and Effect   Scholastic Teaching Resources

Writing A Cause-and-Effect Story

Opening the Lesson

❋ I read aloud the books *If You Give a Moose a Muffin* (a companion book to *If You Give a Pig a Pancake*) and *Fortunately*. After comparing and contrasting the two books, I ask my students which graphic organizer from pages 45 and 46 they would use to graph the causes and effects in *If You Give a Moose a Muffin*. (the Chain Reaction graphic organizer)

❋ Then I ask which graphic organizer they would use to graph the causes and effects in *Fortunately*. Again, they should select the Chain Reaction organizer. I prompt discussion by asking questions such as *"How are the books similar and different? Which book did you prefer and why?"*

Teaching the Lesson

1. Imitating a writing style or story pattern can be a good learning device. Challenge students to write and illustrate their own chain-reaction, cause-and-effect stories based on *If You Give a Moose a Muffin* (each item that the demanding animal receives causes it to want yet another item) or *Fortunately* (something fortunate happens, and then something unfortunate happens).

2. Before students begin writing, go over the rubric on page 52 with them. Hand out a copy of the rubric for students to refer to as they work. (NOTE: They will *not* be assessing their own work; you will.) Emphasize that their stories should be unique. For example, if they chose *Fortunately*, their story cannot be about a birthday party, a crashing airplane, a parachute, a haystack, and so on.

3. As a pre-writing exercise, students should copy and complete a Chain Reaction graphic organizer.

Closing the Lesson

❋ **Kinesthetic:** Extend your students' creativity by having them turn their stories into books, placing each cause-and-effect statement on a single sheet of paper with a colored illustration.

Objective

Students write a story with a sequence of cause-and-effect events that are part of a chain reaction.

Materials

Fortunately by Remy Charlip (Aladdin, 1964), *If You Give a Moose a Muffin* by Laura Numeroff (HarperCollins, 1991), or similar books; construction paper, notebook paper, markers, colored pencils, stapler, glue

Reproducibles

Cause-and-Effect Graphic Organizers 1–2, page 45 (transparency or posters)

Cause-and-Effect Graphic Organizers 3–5, page 46 (transparency or posters)

Cause-and-Effect Story Rubric, page 52 (Make 1 copy for each student.)

Cause-and-Effect Story Rubric

CRITERIA	Incomplete 0	Okay 1	Good 2	Outstanding 3

Assignment | | | | **Score**

1. The story contains at least four different cause-and-effect statements.

2. Each cause-and-effect statement appears on a single sheet of paper with a colored illustration.

3. The story is creative and original.

Structure and Style

4. The story follows the same chain-reaction pattern as the model book.

5. The sentences on each page are complete.

6. Grammar, spelling, punctuation, and capitalization are correct.

Presentation

7. The book is unique. (It may be any shape, size, or color. Be creative! Your book must be bound somehow—strings, staples, and so on.)

8. It looks like a book (including cover with catchy title, illustration, and author's name, title page, and copyright/dedication page).

9. The illustrations are creative.

Here is what I enjoyed about the book:

Here are some suggestions for improvement:

TOTAL SCORE: _____ /27

Comprehension Mini-Lessons: Inference & Cause and Effect   Scholastic Teaching Resources

Fiction Flip Books

Opening the Lesson

✤ This is a good time to discuss which causes and events in a story are the main ones and which are minor. Main events really change the story, while minor events hardly alter the story line. For example, I explain a main cause-and-effect relationship in *Maniac Magee* by Jerry Spinelli like this:

Cause: Maniac was not a prejudiced person. He didn't notice a person's skin color. He treated the East Enders just like the West Enders. He had friends on each side, like Amanda and Grayson. Effect: Because he was not prejudiced, Maniac was able to unite the East Enders with the West Enders. He showed them that they could get along and put a stop to the division that existed between them.

✤ Then I choose a book or story that the whole class has read together and ask small groups to brainstorm to find the main cause-and-effect relationships in that work.

Teaching the Lesson

1. Students will select and read a chapter book, write down five main cause-and-effect relationships from the book, and then create a flip book based on those causes and effects. After students have *elaborated* on the five main causes in a rough draft, they'll transfer the causes and effects to a flip book. (NOTE: It's very important that students elaborate on each cause and effect because they'll be sharing their flip books. One of the benefits of the flip books is that they encourage other students to read the chapter book.)

2. Here's how to make the flip books:

Step 1: Use an inch ruler and scissors to measure and trim the five sheets of paper to create the following sizes: 8½ by 3 inches, 8 ½ by 5 inches, 8 ½ by 7 inches, 8 ½ by 9 inches, and 8 ½ by 11 inches (no cut necessary). Align the sheets of paper at the top (8 ½ inches in width); the longest

Objective

Students write five main cause-and-effect relationships from a novel to use as the basis for a flip book.

Materials

inch ruler, scissors, stapler, a variety of trade books*; five sheets of 8 ½- by 11-inch paper (light colors or white) for each student

* You might want to consult with your school librarian and have students choose from the librarian's selection of books.

sheet is on the bottom and the shortest sheet is on top.

Step 2: Staple in three places along the top to bind the sheets of paper.

Step 3: With a ruler, draw a horizontal line to divide each sheet into two sections. Each line should be drawn so that it aligns with the bottom of the previous page.

Step 4: The first page (3 by 8 1/2 inches) will have the title of the book and name of the author written above the line and Cause #1 written below the line. The second page (5 by 8 1/2 inches) will have Effect #1 written above the line and Cause #2 written below the line, and so on. As each cause page is lifted, the corresponding effect will be revealed on the page underneath. Effect #5 will be written on the back of the book.

Step 5: Wherever there is extra white space, draw an illustration. "Seeing" a story always enhances the meaning for the reader.

3. Remember, elaboration and neatness are important.

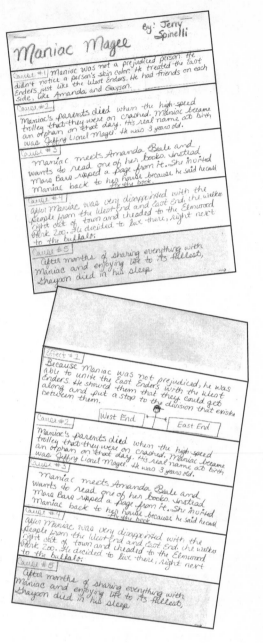

Closing the Lesson

Use one or more of these activities to wrap up the mini-lesson.

✱ **Auditory:** Have students share the two most important causes and effects from their books with the rest of the class.

✱ **Journal:** Have students record their thoughts about the following questions: Which of the books most interested you? Which books would you like to read, and why? How did the flip books help you choose?

Test-Taking Format

Opening the Lesson

❧ To sharpen my students' cause-and-effect detection skills, I have them play a rousing game of "My Turn, Your Turn." A game consists of four rounds.

❧ Pairs of students play the game. The first partner gives a cause and the second partner must give a resulting effect. The order of causes and effects are switched in alternating rounds. (NOTE: The causes and effects in each round do not have to be related.) Here are some examples.

> **Round One**
>
> First partner: "Cause: It rained today. Your turn."
>
> Second partner: "Effect: The soccer game was canceled."
>
> **Round Two**
>
> First partner: "Effect: The North won the Civil War. Your turn."
>
> Second partner: "Cause: The North had more factories."

❧ For the second game, partners switch roles. You can keep this going as long as you want to, but I find that two games are usually enough. Students really have to think fast in this game—and yes, some of the answers can get really outlandish! That's okay as long as the partners are able to relate the causes and effects.

Teaching the Lesson

1. Now that students have proven that they can supply missing causes and effects, it's time to see if they can determine the causes and effects in a test-taking format.

2. Distribute copies of the Tsunamis passage. Read aloud the passage, or ask a volunteer to do so.

3. Display the Cause-and-Effect Graphic Organizer poster or transparency for the Traditional graphic organizer. Use it to model how to answer the first question. I might say something like this:

"The first question is, What causes a tsunami? When I skim the passage, I see the word caused *in the first paragraph. It says that an undersea*

Objective

Students identify causes and effects in sample test passages.

Reproducibles

Tsunamis, page 57 (Make 1 copy for each student.)

Asian Eels, page 58 (Make 1 copy for each student.)

Cause-and-Effect Graphic Organizers 3–5, page 46 (transparency or poster)

earthquake causes a tsunami. Undersea earthquakes is one of the answer choices; it's answer choice C. Just to be sure, I'll see if I can eliminate the other choices. The last paragraph states that high and low tides never cause tsunamis. I know from the first paragraph that seismic sea waves are tsunamis. And there are no scientific experiments mentioned in the passage. I'm positive that the answer is C."

4. Read aloud the remaining questions and answer choices. Have students draw and complete copies of the Traditional graphic organizer to help them answer the questions. Call on volunteers to answer the questions and explain their thinking processes.

Closing the Lesson

Use one or more of these activities to wrap up the mini-lesson:

✤ **Assessment:** Direct students to practice on their own with the Asian Eels passage. Make sure students are able to answer both questions which ask them to identify causes and questions which ask them to identify effects.

✤ **Students Working Together:** Let pairs or small groups of students choose short passages from their science or social studies textbooks. Have them write two or three cause-and-effect test questions for the passage. Then have pairs or groups exchange and answer the questions.

Answers
Tsunamis, page 57: 1. C; 2. A; 3. A
Asian Eels, page 58: 1. A; 2. D; 3. C

Cause-and-Effect Passage Practice

Tsunamis

Put away those surfboards! Even the best surfer wouldn't want to ride a tsunami. The name *tsunami* comes from the Japanese language. It is the scientific term for a seismic sea wave—a giant wave that is caused by an undersea earthquake.

Scientists believe that tsunamis occur when an earthquake lifts or tilts the ocean floor. The earthquake creates very long waves that speed across the sea. Tsunamis can travel at speeds of up to five hundred miles an hour. The waves grow in height as they approach the shore. Some monster-sized tsunamis can tower sixty feet or higher above the ocean's surface.

Tsunamis are sometimes called tidal waves, but that name is misleading. High and low tides never cause tsunamis. Only earthquakes or volcanic eruptions do. But by any name, tsunamis can be very dangerous. Hawaii has been hit by over forty tsunamis!

Choose the best answer.

1. What causes a tsunami?

(A) high and low tides

(B) seismic sea waves

(C) undersea earthquakes

(D) scientific earthquakes

2. Volcanic eruptions can cause—

(A) huge waves in the ocean.

(B) dangerous thunderstorms.

(C) temperature changes.

(D) changes in high and low tides.

3. One of the worst effects of a tsunami is most likely—

(A) major flooding.   (C) burning buildings.

(B) constant rainfall.   (D) not being able to surf.

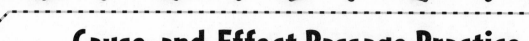

Cause-and-Effect Passage Practice

Asian Eels

Large numbers of Asian eels are eating the small fish in ponds near Atlanta, Georgia. Without this important food source, the bigger fish in the ponds may starve to death. To make matters worse, this eel problem could spread to other areas.

The Asian eel is native to Southeast Asia and Australia. How did these invaders get into ponds in the United States? Scientist John Biagi believes that pet owners put them there. Baby Asian eels look like colorful ribbons. As adults, however, they grow to three feet in length. Biagi says that fish-tank owners who didn't realize they were raising such large creatures set the adults free.

It may sound kind, but releasing the eels into the wild was the wrong thing to do, says Biagi. "The eels upset the ecosystem and may cause some native species to die out in the ponds."

Choose the best answer.

1. Why did pet owners put their Asian eels into ponds?

(A) The eels reached lengths of up to three feet.

(B) They looked like colorful ribbons in the water.

(C) They hoped to upset the ecosystem.

(D) They wanted the eels to eat the fish in the ponds.

2. The bigger fish are in danger of starving to death because—

(A) they do not like to eat Asian eels.

(B) their main food source is not reproducing.

(C) the plants in the ponds are dying.

(D) Asian eels are eating their food.

3. What is the most damaging effect of the eels being released into the wild?

(A) They could spread to other areas.

(B) They are eating the small fish.

(C) They upset the ecosystem.

(D) They belong in Southeast Asia.

Comprehension Mini-Lessons: Inference & Cause and Effect   Scholastic Teaching Resources

Putting It All Together: CHAINS

Preparing for the Project

❋ I tell my students that they'll be learning about a research method that will help them analyze and think about solutions to problems. These problems can range from situations they encounter at school to world problems.

❋ To introduce the CHAINS method, I like to use a problem or a behavior that my class is currently struggling with, such as one student speaking negatively about another student. I display the CHAINS Research Template transparency and explain that we'll be analyzing the results of a particular kind of behavior that often occurs at school.

❋ Then I go through each step of the CHAINS method for the problem. An abbreviated sample response is given below. You may choose to model the sample, or you may want to encourage students to participate.

C – Choose a situation: talking about another student behind his or her back

H – Have possible outcomes listed:
  • hurt feelings if he or she finds out
  • reputation might be ruined
  • comments could be false

A – Advance one of the outcomes: reputation might be ruined

I – Indicate chain of events: reputation might be ruined
  • other students start to make fun of him or her
  • damages student's self-esteem and makes him or her insecure
  • depression or anger

N – Note cause-and-effect relationships:
  • Talking behind someone's back can lead to low self-esteem and depression.
  • Low self-esteem can cause a person to talk about someone else.

S – Solutions: Someone who talks about other people may really feel insecure about himself or herself. If someone talks badly about someone else, say that you don't want to hear it. Try to engage him/her in a positive discussion.

Objective

Students analyze the cause-and-effect relationship of an event by using the CHAINS research method.

Materials

newspaper articles and other information resources

Reproducibles

CHAINS: Cause-and-Effect Research Method, page 61 (Make 1 copy for each student.)

CHAINS Research Template, page 62 (Make 1 transparency and 2 copies for each student.)

CHAINS Student Response Sheet, page 63 (Make 2 copies for each student.)

Introducing the Project

1. For this final project, students will use the CHAINS method to analyze another school topic and a current world, country, state, or community topic. At the end of the project, they will have completed two CHAINS Research Templates with their analyses. Distribute the copies of the CHAINS Cause-and-Effect Research Method and CHAINS Research Templates to students.

2. In order to help students choose a world, country, state, or community problem to analyze, have them do the following for homework: cut out a newspaper article on a topic of interest or talk to an older family member about a topic. If students get stuck in choosing topics, encourage them to brainstorm topics in small groups or provide them with a list of sample behaviors and current events. Some topics are suggested below.

Possible School Topics	**Possible Community or World Topics**
stealing or lying	pollution (air, water, ground)
cheating	natural disasters (tornadoes, hurricanes, storms, floods, earthquakes)
not studying for tests or doing homework	
adding or removing a particular class	farming and ranching
changing the length of the school year	nutrition and health

3. Students will also need other resources to complete their CHAINS analysis of the world topic. Make sure everyone has access to resources such as newspapers, magazines, reference books, and the Internet.

Assessing the Project

✿ When students have completed their two analyses, pass out the completed copies of the CHAINS Research Template and the CHAINS Student Response Sheet to groups of four students. (NOTE: Make sure that none of the group members gets his or her own template.) When you say, "Go," students will read over the CHAINS templates and then add their own solutions and cause-and-effect relationships to the CHAINS Student Response Sheet. After students complete that set, repeat the process until each group has reviewed four templates.

✿ Repeat the activity with the set of community or world topics. This activity takes two class periods, but it will help students understand about causes and effects and solutions to more problems.

CHAINS: Cause-and-Effect Research Method

C – Choose a situation (a problem or a topic).
H – Have possible outcomes listed.
A – Advance one of the outcomes. Pick one that interests you. Be specific!
I – Indicate the chain of events.
N – Note as many other cause-and-effect relationships you can
think of that are related to your situation.
S – Solutions: Suggest solutions to the situation.

C air pollution

H harmful to people, animals, and environment; the cost of higher tech-
nological growth and production

A harmful to people: asthma

I Smog can cause asthma. People with asthma need medical treatment.
Treatment is expensive. Treatment may cause people to miss school or
work. Schools and workplaces are affected.

N air pollution (cause)/acid rain (effect)
acid rain/ruins buildings
smog in cities/causes lung problems or allergies
smog/causes animals to suffer
more factories/create more air pollution
more factories/create more products

S Build fewer factories. Place regulations on factory output of pollution.
Encourage carpooling in cities. Set out air pollution detectors so people
with asthma can read level of pollutants in the air. Encourage people
to live in rural areas. Grow more plants in cities to help clean the air.

CHAINS Research Template

C – Choose a situation (a problem or a topic).

H – Have possible outcomes listed.

A – Advance one of the outcomes. Pick one that interests you. Be specific!

I – Indicate the chain of events.

N – Note as many other cause-and-effect relationships you can think of that are related to your situation.

S – Solutions: Suggest solutions to the situation.

C _____

H _____

_____

_____

A _____

I _____

_____

_____

_____

N _____

_____

_____

_____

_____

S _____

_____

_____

_____

Comprehension Mini-Lessons: Inference & Cause and Effect   Scholastic Teaching Resources

CHAINS Student Response Sheet

1. Situation: _____

Additional causes and effects: _____

_____

_____

Additional solutions: _____

_____

_____

2. Situation: _____

Additional causes and effects: _____

_____

_____

Additional solutions: _____

_____

_____

3. Situation: _____

Additional causes and effects: _____

_____

_____

Additional solutions: _____

_____

_____

4. Situation: _____

Additional causes and effects: _____

_____

_____

Additional solutions: _____

_____

_____

Teacher Resources

Beech, Linda Ward. *Ready-to-Go Reproducibles: Short Reading Passages and Graphic Organizers to Build Comprehension (Grades 4–5 and Grades 6–8).* New York: Scholastic, Inc., 2001.

Billmeyer, Rachel and Mary Lee Barton. *Teaching Reading in the Content Areas: If Not Me, Then Who?* Aurora, CO: McREL, 1998.

Bixby, M. *Prove It: Whole Language Strategies for Secondary Students.* Katonah, New York: Richard Owen Publishing Co., 1988.

Howard, Mary. *Helping Your Struggling Students Be More Successful Readers (Grades 4–6).* Tulsa, OK: Reading Connections, 2003.*

Robb, Laura. *Reading Strategies That Work.* New York: Scholastic, Inc., 1995.

Wilhelm, Jeffrey D. *Action Strategies for Deepening Comprehension.* New York: Scholastic, Inc., 2002.

Wilhelm, Jeffrey D. *Improving Comprehension With Think-Aloud Strategies.* New York: Scholastic, Inc., 2001.

* This book is available at *http://www.drmaryhoward.com.*